Thank you for being my dad.

_____

_____

_____

_____

Because of You, Dad

Written by Kobi Yamada · Illustrated by Natalie Russell

Because of you, life is filled with
laughter, stories, and adventures.

I learned to put my heart
into everything I do.

You didn't just tell me
how to be a good person,
you showed me.

Because of you, Dad, I've always
had someone to look up to.

So many of my favorite
memories are with you.

You made time for me, even when
it wasn't easy to find the time.

Because of you, Dad, I know what it's like
to have someone who sees the best in me.

You believed in me before I believed in myself.

I can still hear you cheering me on.

Because of you, I have someone who shares
my hopes and supports my dreams.

I feel like I can go anywhere

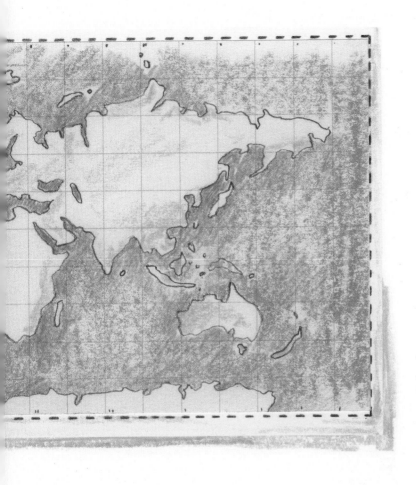

and do anything.

And I know there will always be open arms
waiting for me, welcoming me home.

Because of you, Dad, I know who I am.

And even if I don't say it,
I'm thankful for you every day.

Because of you, I am me.

COMPENDIUM.

live inspired

Written by: Kobi Yamada

Illustrated by: Natalie Russell

Edited by: Kristin Eade

Art Directed by: Megan Gandt Guansing

ISBN: 978-1-970147-25-4

2nd printing. Printed in China with soy inks on FSC®-Mix certified paper. A032103002

Create meaningful moments with gifts that inspire.

CONNECT WITH US

live-inspired.com | sayhello@compendiuminc.com

@compendiumliveinspired
#compendiumliveinspired